MY SOUL'S COMPASS

Poems of Healing and Insight

Christine M. Tozzo

©2024 by Christine M. Tozzo

All rights reserved. No part of this book may be reproduced or transmitted in any form or by any means, electronic or mechanical, including photocopying, recording or by any information storage and retrieval system without permission in writing from the publisher.

About the Author

My journey to writing this book of poems has taken a long and winding road through my life. I never believed in my gift and kept most poems to myself...only reading one for specific causes. One day in the 90's I was asked to submit a poem to a magazine...and I did with Family Trees. I came home one day to a full mailbox of people from all over the U.S. telling me I helped heal their family. The phone did not stop for months and I personally got to speak to many. Some brought it to a family reunion or mailed it to a relative who was estranged. I was in awe of the passion and compassion that the poem resonated in their hearts and souls. Shortly after that I was asked to write a poem for a convention...after reading it to a standing ovation...young priest came on stage and said "Lady. You sure are a tough act to follow"... The poem is Peace Love and Understanding....and finally here I am... an author of a book of poems. Almost 30 years later!

Intention

The first poem I ever wrote was for P.J....our 15-year-old neighbor who lost his battle with an enlarged heart.

He was an amazing young man and best friends with my two boys.

Their father, my husband, died a few months before P.J and the devastation was overwhelming. I remember reading the poem...which was handwritten...to a group of his family and friends. The emotions were overwhelming and their gratitude was uplifting and heartwarming. I did not believe it was a gift...more like a God Wink to help through the pain.

Table of Contents

Clouds and Clarity 11
- Yesterday, Today and Tomorrow… 12
- Dance of the Souls 14
- Am I Enough? 15
- Questions 16
- Circle Dance 17
- Learn To Dance 18
- The Dance of Life 19
- Notes 21

Family Breaks and Bonds 22
- Family Trees 23
- Gossip 25
- It's All Relative! 26
- Think Twice…. Be Nice 27
- Words and Wisdom 28
- The Hidden Child 29
- Chosen 31
- Perverse Psychology 32
- Notes 34

The World and Salvation 35

Confusion and His Words 37

The Edge of the World…9-11 38

The Past, Present and Future 39

The Calling... 40

Notes 41

Loneliness and Grace 42

Crossroads 43

Opened Eyes and Hearts 45

Inner Dimension 47

Where The Road Bends 49

Dance with Angels 50

Depression and Salvation 51

Eye to Eye 52

Notes 53

Heaven and Earth 54

Angels Among Us 55

Afterglow 58

Lost and Found… 59

The Signs… 60

Speak to Me 61

Wonder 62

Notes 63

The Love of Our Furry Friends 64

The Bond and Beyond… 64
Rainbow Bridge Angels... 67
The Teachings of Hope... 68
My Name Is Khalessi.... 70
Life at the Pound... 72
Senior Moments.. 73
Notes... 74

Hope for the Misunderstood 75
The Homeless Prayer… 75
Indifference.. 78
Peace, Love, And Understanding 79
Reaching Out 80
The Lonely Place… 81
Expectations and Realizations 82
Giving Hands and Hearts… 83
Notes... 84

Ecology and Change 85
Stop, Look and Listen! 87
The Earth's Prayer... 88
The Winds of Change… 89
The Eye of the Storm 90
Poisoned Promises 91
Notes... 92

Frustration and Realization 93
    Black and White 94
    The War 96
    Pathways of Life 97
    The Battle Zone 98
    Life's Lessons 99
    Lifeline 100
    One Day at a Time… 101
    Time 102
    Up, Up and Away…. 103
    When I'm Old and Gray… 104
    If You Believe.... 105
    Notes 106

Clouds and Clarity

Yesterday, Today and Tomorrow…

Yesterday is already gone, swept away by dark of night

There is no way to get it back and change a wrong to right

Regrets and tears won't undo a thing but if you start anew

The dawning of today'as the chance to do all that you can do

With each second, every moment...you can make the best

Of what the day holds in store...no time to stop and rest

For when today is ended and tomorrow's sun is on the rise

We know not what the future holds...pain or a sweet surprise

So focus on the day at hand and let the past and future go

Today we all can make a difference...let your inner beauty show!

Christine M. Tozzo ©2009

Dance of the Souls

They say our souls have danced before in another time and place

We were changed and weightless...and yet we left no trace

Our memory is guarded...yet our souls cannot deny

That some things are so familiar... without a reason why

We try to make connections and try to understand

Never really knowing...that every life is planned

We meet those souls that destiny has set up in our path

Maybe the person of our longing...or a source of pain and wrath

Love can make us happy and anger helps us learn

We can choose to make some changes or let our bridges burn

Learning from every soul we meet...accepting good and bad

Helps us to look inside ourselves and make happy what was sad

Reaching out to every day and knowing we are blessed

Accepting challenges, we face and passing every test

When our time on earth is done we can only smile

Knowing that we did God's will in true Christian style.

Christine M. Tozzo © 1999

Am I Enough?

When I ask this question…it becomes a mystery

Is it what the world sees…. or what I think of me?

When I do God's purpose silently or out loud

Behind closed doors…secretly or in front of a crowd

Can I fill this hole in me with resounding praise?

Or fall into the inner trap with my defeatist ways

All the tapes of long ago and some from yesterday

Seem to win time after time…and just won't go away

I make myself a promise to see me through HIS eyes

It disappears like vapor as my inner child still cries

There is an emptiness I carry to disguise the pain

Frozen in my soul as my teardrops fall like rain

My hope and prayer is to realize we all carry scars inside

But they don't define us…their poison can be cast aside

With God's help and guidance and words of victory

There will be a brighter day…when I believe in the real me!!

Christine M. Tozzo © 2005

Questions

We go through life in a state of confusion

Berating ourselves for the knowledge we lack

Stumbling along chasing each new illusion

With each faltering step we keep looking back

Going over and over each perceived mistake

Hoping magically answers will leap from the sky

Changing course for we know the decisions we make

Are directing our future but we don't know why

All things do happen for reasons unknown

Each path that we travel just part of His plan

Every harvester reaps from the seeds he has sown

You'll reach your goal if you believe that you can

Don't follow another in mindless pursuit

Of a dream that's elusive and so out of reach

Your mind holds the power…your soul reaps the prize

God will give you strength…seeing life though His eyes!

Christine M. Tozzo © 2023

Circle Dance

Why is life so very strange

The more we try, the less we change

Old habits haunt us every day

Too scared to find another way

Around and around we pirouette

In endless circles of regret

We have the power to take a stand

To heed the call of a distant band

Telling us to take a chance

And step outside the circle dance

Our childhood fears we'll shed like cloaks

For life is real…it's not a hoax

We only get one chance to shine

I'll hold your hand if you'll hold mine

We'll make our mark and shine so bright

God's power is our guiding light!

Christine M. Tozzo ©1995

Learn To Dance

We can reach out and take a chance
Or stay alone within our walls
Hear the music…learn to dance
Or wait until the curtain falls

Who's to say what's right or wrong
Which path will lead to Heaven's door
It's the words within the song
That stay with us forever more;

We're all part of a melody
Echoing from soul to soul
Each chord that's played is meant to be
Two hearts in tune the final goal.

Don't be afraid to sing along
Although the words don't make much sense
How will you hear the perfect song?
If your world is all past tense!

      Christine M. Tozzo ©1995

The Dance of Life

In the blink of an eye...in a second of time
All of life changes...without reason or rhyme
All dreams seem to perish...all hope disappears
Life, once so precious...now filled with new fears

God closes doors, but when you look around
You won't believe all the windows you've found
Chance to take notice of the beauty and grace
Of those who reach out to the whole human race

Those not afraid to leave dreams far behind
Then look for some new ones that God helps you find
Hope for a future, not the same as before
Yet always preparing for that next open door

Always keeping in mind that faith is the key
Of accepting each day as it is meant to be

God knows your future and sends you a test
And the strength to go on when you're longing for rest

We all dance through life to our very own song

Sometimes wondering where and why things went wrong

Yet all things do happen for reasons unknown
Like the leaves on a tree, we get shaken and blown

Acknowledge your strengths...you're an army of two
Open your eyes to see what our God can do!

                    Christine M. Tozzo © 1998

Notes

Family Breaks and Bonds

Family Trees

We're born into a family tree
Its roots extend through you and me

Our family's large, the seeds are sown
Each year our family tree has grown

But sometimes branches go astray
From hurtful words of yesterday

And even though the roots go on
The foundation of our family's gone

As we all get on in years
We long to cast aside our fears

And put away our foolish pride
Then gather family to our side

Those who've gone before us all
Will smile in Heaven and heed the call

For us to gather at Heaven's door
The scattered branches rejoined once more!

Christine M. Tozzo © 1995

Gossip

Gossip is a sickness -- that plays with people's minds
Helps them forget their troubles…and render's them so blind

As to whether it's their business to report and to convey
To anyone who'all listen to what they have to say

Like the game of telephone, the words they twist and turn
Is it your life or is it mine…when will people ever learn?

There's two sides to every story…words conveniently left out
Loads of misconceptions… beyond a shadow of a doubt

So before you spread some gossip…look yourself straight in the eye
And say: "Is this my business…do I have the right to pry?"

With these questions answered, I am hoping you will know
Even if you think you're perfect…you have no stones to throw!!

Christine M. Tozzo © 1989

It's All Relative!

We can just go round and round,
pointing fingers at each other

Until one day at last we've found
we're just different from each other

I will never see things your way
you will never see things mine

I just hope there will be one day
we can reach the bottom line

When all the anger's said and done
one thing that I know is true

This is not a game that can be won
it all comes down to me and you

Why can't we just put down our armor
and forget the things we've said

Let go of the pride and drama
and concentrate on life ahead?

Christine M. Tozzo © 1995

Think Twice…. Be Nice

You can't unring a bell and you can't unsay a word
Can't erase the hurtful sting from what you just heard

Words said in anger are really said in fear
Loss of control and selfishness suddenly appear

Lashing out to anyone who needs to take the blame
Uncontrolled and unbridled….it always feels the same

It is meant to bring another soul into your angry world
Emotions at a fever pitch … unleashed and swept and swirled

The person on the receiving end has a choice to make
Try to pacify the situation…though their efforts might be fake

Or choose to keep their pride and not enter the fray
Listen to the tirade in silence and simply walk away

It truly does not matter…in a Christian state of mind
We need to speak with kindness and often we will find

We get more respect and help when we take a different view
If we stop and ask ourselves "what would Jesus do?"

So when you find yourself at the receiving end of condemnation
Let God's light in and disregard words of anger and frustration

Remind yourself that bitter words come from a broken soul
Pray for their circumstance…God is always in control!

Christine M. Tozzo © 2016

Words and Wisdom

Words bounce around in my brain filled with defeat
I feel shattered from the fight to become complete

The demons from my inner soul try to take a stand
I can only wait and pray for God to unleash His plan
I lay quietly in the silence as the tear drops fall like rain
Reliving all my past mistakes with complete distain

Trust that has been shattered …betrayals of my life
Attached to me day and night…filling me with strife
When the storm is at my door and I'm fighting not to drown
I try to find God's truth to raise me to higher ground

In the midst of the fight He always finds a simple way
To lift me up from the despair's depth each and every day
I recall my inner child fighting just to be loved and heard
I focus on all the good I have done and memorize each word

The thank you's for my generosity …the difference I make
Those who love me unconditionally…and filter out the fake
The devil carves a path but God blocks His point of view

So my defeat is only fleeting and I fight to see what's true
Another day is dawning…a deep breath and off I go
Praying for peace and silence…and God's divine plan to flow!

Christine M. Tozzo © 2024

The Hidden Child

You can't feel her agony
Shattered trust that you can't see
Darkest secrets no one knows
Silent as the teardrop flows
She lives in fear…too scared to tell
Her childhood days a living hell

Go and hide inside your mind
Close your eyes -- pretend you are blind
You will be saved on one sweet day
Free to be a child at play

Why can't we hear her silent cries?
See beyond her childish lies
To find the little girl inside
She runs but knows that she can't hide
Listen hard and you will hear
Her tiny heart that pounds with fear

Break her from the chains of hell
Let her know it's safe to tell
Childhood scars don't fade away
Together we must find a way
To help her set those demons free
I know because that child was me.

Christine M. Tozzo © 1996

Chosen

We are born into this world into different kinds of families
Some are wonderful and loving, others simply cannot see

What a child needs in life to grow up with confidence
To be all that they can be...not live life in pretense

God always has a plan when a child's world has gone astray
He finds the perfect parents to step in and light the way

The new life is set in motion and that child of yesteryear
Blossoms like a flower and grows more beautiful and dear

Free to choose her path ahead and given an opportunity
To be a light in other's lives just as she was now set free

It is a blessing from God when pain and heartache turn around
As He sets you on a wondrous path with your feet on solid ground

Others may not understand your journey and have a different view
It truly does not matter...it's between your parents, God and you!!

Christine M. Tozzo © 2015

Perverse Psychology

Fear once etched my face

Left there by his disgrace

It is gone without a trace

A smile is in it's place;

The shame was not my own

I was a child and he was grown

All along he should have known

He'd reap the pain that once was sown;

I was under his control

Every day, pain took its toll

But I would not give him my soul

He never reached his final goal;

I've left my abuser far behind

Yet, every day I find

That society is blind

To a sick, sadistic mind;

Masquerading as a friend

The charade is just pretend

Breaking trust that cannot mend

We must stop this awful trend;

Every step along the way

God is with me every day

When I close my eyes to pray

I know my smile is here to stay!

                        Christine M. Tozzo © 1997

Notes

The World and Salvation

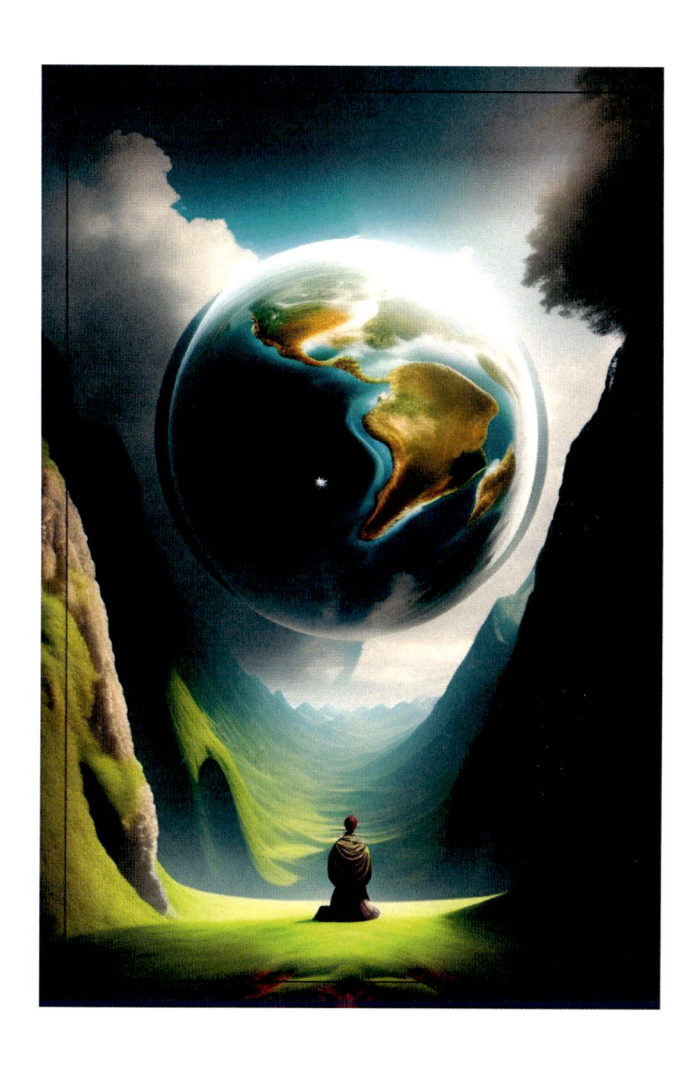

Confusion and His Words

Have you ever felt the sting of the wavering universe
Aware the world around us is working in reverse

What blossomed yesterday is tossed out with the trash
When life feels like a roller coaster that's about to crash

We pray to God for guidance because we've lost our way
Stumbling around...so overwhelmed...confusion every day

Like a brass ring on a merry-go-round...it's so hard to grasp
How the world has gone astray and her people cannot clasp

Where to turn...what to believe. And how to make it right
Through the darkness and pain when will we see the light?

Where are the rainbows and sunshine that used to fill the void
How can we find that inner peace and know what to avoid

We pray His words in the bible hoping they will light our soul
Try to spread love and kindness...as depression takes its toll

Let's pray for peace on earth and for God's battles to be won
What life holds in store...we don't know...but His will be done!

Christine Tozzo © 2024

The Edge of the World…9-11

On that beautiful Tuesday morning underneath a bright blue sky
The bustling of New York City was just the same as days gone by

When the towers were invaded life as we knew it went away
The threats foretold of evil's grip the world changed that fateful day

The suffering seemed so endless…and the future very unclear
We tried to make sense of the heartache…and tried to contain the fear

What were the lessons learned from the events of that cowardly act
When our nation was tested completely…yet leaving our faith intact

We fell as one to our knees…not in defeat but in fervent prayer
Then stood tall…shoulder to shoulder…helping and doing our share

Out from the rubble, the horrendous depiction of all the lives that were lost

There was no human way to measure what our complacency cost

The tales of heroes and miracles amid all the sorrow and grief
Touched the hearts of the world and our nation with surreal disbelief

At the end of the search and recovery and then the final death toll
We as a nation knew the demons had not accomplished their final goal

Those who lost their lives flew like Angels …. up on a Heavenly flight
And those of us left behind have learned and will never again lose sight

Of what our freedom and flag stand for…and the strength we carry inside
We must remain focused and certain God is always our prevailing guide!

Christine M. Tozzo © 2001

The Past, Present and Future

Each day the sun rises and then it sets
On lives filled with promises and with regrets
Words yet unspoken that long to be said
Dreams yet unfilled that dance in your head

Life passes quickly if you keep looking back
Reliving mistakes that keep you off track
There is always a future…that much we know
To learn by mistakes…is how we all grow

By righting a wrong and touching a heart
And spanning a distance too long apart

Your heart and your mind will soon realize
The years have been fruitful and left you more wise
To follow those dreams without guilt or blame
Not stuck in a present that is always the same
Just open your eyes and you'll surely see
Your soul knows the future and what's meant to be.

Christine M. Tozzo © 1998

The Calling...

God has a plan for our lives long before our birth

Guided by His loving hands on our walk upon the earth

We sometimes fail to heed the call and try a different way

Wondering why life seems off key when we go astray

Our insight into our future...suddenly comes into view

When we are enlightened...we know what we want to do

Though the roads we travel...we may have obstacles and wrath

If we listen to our inner voice...we will stay focused on our path

We each have our gifts to give and a void that must be filled

Spread love and compassion and wipe away each teardrop spilled

Sometimes a person spews hate and wrath and we step away

It's protection of our heart and mind so we don't go astray

So listen to your inner voice and keep your head up high

Seek shelter from the negative... god's pure love will show you why!

Christine Tozzo © 2024

Notes

Loneliness and Grace

Crossroads

When the threads of life start to unravel

Its fabric has worn thin and bare

There are only two roads you can travel

One holds hope and the other despair

You can sit yourself down on the roadside

Wondering which way to go

Or journey with God as your guide

In a short while you will know

When you find yourself at a crossroad

Remember that God knows what's best

When you pray, He will lighten your load

Give your body and soul time to rest

Choosing hope gives you something to live for

By counting your blessings each day

You'll learn how to turn less into more

All He asks is to show you the way!

      Christine M. Tozzo ©1998

Opened Eyes and Hearts

In the dark times of our lives…when we have lost our way
There's a promise that we cling to guiding us as we pray

Jesus walked upon the earth as a simple, mortal man
Travelling down a winding path…all according to God's plan

He sent his only son to be a beacon in the darkest night
His suffering and painful death brought us to the light

Our sins were forgiven but deep in our hearts we know
God's wish is for us to be sentries for our souls to grow

Let us rise as he rose to fight the evil in the world
Make a difference in the dark as God's light is unfurled

We see inhumanity and unrighteous people do their deeds
Stepping over those they could help with some simple need

We hear prejudice and condemnation instead of sweet unity
And pray for God to touch bitter hearts and somehow make them see

Jesus sacrificed for us and we owe the same for all mankind
Keeping vigilant eyes on the cross in the hope that we can find

Compassion, love and kindness in the hearts of those we see
Crushing out the bitterness…as we all fall on bended knee

Let us live like Jesus…and reveal the promise from long ago
We will light the world through his eyes…let His love overflow

When our time on earth is ended…and we look back at our path
Grateful we had the strength and grace to follow his epitaph!

Christine M. Tozzo © 2017

Inner Dimension

When conflict tears at your soul

You feel weary with no time to rest

When everything's out of control

That's when God is sending a test

If you go to your "inner dimension"

Find the balance and peace in your heart

Let go of the stress and the tension

That for so long has torn you apart

You can walk, once again, in the sunshine

Chase the clouds and the gloom far away

You'll find rainbows and they are a sure sign

It is God who has shown you the way

All things in this world have a reason

We must learn as we go along

Every second, each day, every season

We lament all the things that are wrong

If we believe that our souls have been given

The chance to change wrong into right

All the anger with which we've been driven

Will suddenly fade out of sight.

                        Christine M. Tozzo © 1996

Where The Road Bends

We go through life with our hopes up high
Preparing for roadblocks but with a sad sigh

The road we thought was bringing us to the light
A future of happiness feeling loved day and night

What we forget is our path is what we wish for
But other souls interfere and we must endure

The bends in the road may be crooked and worn
We can traverse them with ease or be forlorn

If a ripple or strong wind blocks our view
The bends might be the key to something new

So every morning and night in your life
Discard the sadness and ever present strife

There are others worse off and when they pray
They only hope for essentials if just for a day

Let's light the fire of compassion and service
Bringing hope to a world that makes us nervous

At the days end you will sleep satisfied
For tending to a human who really tried

You opened their roadblock if only for a while
Thank you for a heart that brought a soul a smile

Christine Tozzo © 2024

Dance with Angels

They have gone to dance with Angels
They have reached and touched the sky
Wearing golden wings of Angels
They will teach our souls to fly

Although our hearts are saddened
We need to simply close our eyes
Feel the magic and be gladdened
A spirit lives and never dies

Feel each warm embrace in sunshine
Gentle breezes send a kiss
Look for rainbows as a sure sign
They dwell in God's house of bliss

We should not despair their leaving
Bask in the blue skies…not the gray
There seems no respite from our grieving
But we will meet again one day

Let's not waste one precious moment
As they guide us from above
Cast out the pain and torment
And accept each gift of peace and love.

Christine M. Tozzo © 1996

Depression and Salvation

The day begins with a heavy sigh
Hold back the tears. No time to cry

The tasks before me are a heavy load
I'll work till I feel I could explode

I look around and no one is there
To lighten the loads that I bear

When I step outside I feel free
Time to feed the creatures who welcome me

The deer. The birds the old barn cats
Who prefer store bought to mice and rats

The amazing beauty of the rising sun
The sunsets glow when the day is done

I remember that I am truly blessed
I've earned the chance to get some rest!

Christine M. Tozzo © 2024

Eye to Eye

There is much we can learn from each person eyes

Are they kindly or selfish…egotistic or wise?

Are the words we hear spoken heartfelt and true

Do you feel that they really care about you?

When you look eye-to eye the truth will appear

And the true inner person become crystal clear

By looking beyond each person's smile

You will find who's been hiding there all the while

Do not judge another by their outer facade

Just believe in those people whose souls honor God!

Christine M. Tozzo © 2014

Notes

Heaven and Earth

Angels Among Us

There are forces working in this world we cannot explain

We sometimes close our hearts to them and only see the pain

They come to us in whispers and we simply fail to hear

So lost in our sadness we can't feel that they are near

There are Angels all around us sent to each of us by God

For every time they're needed they assume a new facade

Like a good friend far away who calls when you feel down

Or a stranger on the street who smiles despite your frown

Have you ever made decisions when your mind was so confused?

And have it be the right ones…that's God's Angels being used

In this life we have a journey and our spirit learns and grows

We bear our pain and heartache and the grief that overflows

Troubles make us stronger and we see life through different eyes

As we reach out to each other through dark and stormy skies

As our Angels walk among us we ALL can do the work they do

Open up your heart and mind to share the light inside of you!

Christine M. Tozzo © 2001

Afterglow

When you think of me do you imagine my soul

Flying up to the Heavens…free of its earthly role?

Do you picture my body as broken and gone?

Is the image too vivid...is it hard to go on?

Let me tell you my story…let me ease your mind

The place I have gone to is peaceful and kind

There are Angels around me with beauty and grace

I have reached Heaven and it'as a beautiful place

The body you once knew no longer is here

I live in your memory and that's where I'll appear

You cannot feel me or touch me, I know

Close your eyes to feel the power of my afterglow

Someday you'll be with me, please know it's true

Until then I'll be here keeping watch over you.

                        Christine M. Tozzo © 2005

Lost and Found…

When a loved one has departed we say that they are "lost"
Our grieving hearts want them back…no matter what the cost

Yet, if we, as Christians realize that they have been found
We can picture them in Heaven…walking on God's holy ground

All the memories they have left behind….no one can erase
In time we let go of the grief… allowing peace to fill its place

All of life's ups and downs…the heartaches toils and grief
Are washed away on that one day as we cling to our belief

Remembering them in happy times and the gifts they bestowed
On all those who met them…and all the love that overflowed

Grieving may seem like a river…flowing so deep and wide
Never meant to bring us down…. but to open us up inside

Our God may close a door…but in the blinking of an eye
Your heart will know the answers to all the times you asked Him "why?"

Our lives are set in motion from that moment of our birth
God knows the path we'll follow on our walk upon the earth

Love them as you always have and bask in what you know
They are closer than we think… healed in God's afterglow!

Christine M. Tozzo © 2016

The Signs….

When a loved one has departed and we are mired in grief
We hold tight to our memories and cling to our belief

Knowing their soul lives within a different dimension
Their love transcends the distance with sweet Godly intention

Yet, have you ever noticed that when a loved one goes away
Our daily lives see signs if we are open every day

It could be a bird, a feather or a beautiful butterfly
A penny gleaming on the ground as we are walking by

It could be an apparition of a subtle golden glow
Like God's hand has touched us…and somehow you just know

A perfect song on the radio just as we turn it on
Reminding us of their LIFE not just that they are gone

We might smell a fragrance as a familiar memory
Of the love shared between us and suddenly we see

They are closer then we think and the comfort they impart
Is what I choose to carry every day within my heart

Love never dies…and one day we will meet again
Let's open up our eyes and ears to receive their signs till then!

Christine M. Tozzo © 2016

Speak to Me

God, I watched him suffer - I know You saw him, too
I begged for intervention - for a sign, a touch, a clue;

But there was only silence - You did not hear me speak
As the days and months rolled by - and he grew more frail and weak;

The day he died, You answered - I felt You very near
I knew he was in Heaven and I had nothing more to fear;

"Why did You wait so long, God, why now instead of then?"
 "For man's last earthly gift," He said, "is to suffer for all men;"

"He knew I was there with him - I did not turn away
I've heard each word you've spoken, and prayed day after day;"

"His suffering has ended - he'll help watch over you
And wait for you in Heaven - until your life is through!"

Christine M. Tozzo © 1995

Wonder

It's okay to wonder about what lies up ahead
Longing for the best in life. But filled with fear and dread

Anticipating what can go wrong each and every day
When God opens a path you still can't find your way

Memories of younger years when life was compromised
With many hurts and betrayals. Reliving all the lies

You cannot move forward if you keep longing for what you lack
Reliving all the inner pains which keep you so off track

God is at the helm through every stormy road and sea
You need to dive through trials so you can be set free

Life is what you make it...even though some things are hard
God wants to take your cares away...they're for him to discard

In the tunnel you travelled suddenly the end comes into view
Proof through all the ups and downs that you can renew

True faith in yourself and God... so take each day as it unwinds
You'll see you are safe and loved...filled with light and signs!

Christine Tozzo ©2024

Notes

The Love of Our Furry Friends

The Bond and Beyond...

God's domesticated creatures have a gift that's quite unique
They can let you know they love you even though they cannot speak

With a tail that wags in greeting or a purr that melts your heart
They let you know they've missed you...whenever you're apart

A sweet bond of love created with a Master's gentle hand
A unity of spirit...a connection that was planned

Yet, they cannot stay forever and when it is their time to leave
A broken hearted owner is left to wonder and to grieve

Have they found God's greener pastures where they can romp and play?
Will their kind and gentle spirit return another day?

They've left paw prints on your heart, ones not quickly filled
An aching deep inside and so many teardrops spilled

One day another furry friend seems to call you from afar
Loving eyes seems so familiar and help ease the deepest scar

The bond, once again, grows quickly...and somehow you just know
This was no coincidence...and your heart tells you so!!

Christine M. Tozzo © 1998

Rainbow Bridge Angels....

God prepares many souls to assist our pets in letting go
Of this world's aches and pains and leaving those who love them so

The decision is so bittersweet and it's hard to carry through
The ending of a friendship and send them to live the life they knew

Free to run and play and roam when they cross the bridge and see
Others who have gone before…happy and running free

Those left behind feel the void...longing for just one more day
To hug, give kisses and take long walks...but most of all to play

So we thank those angels who give our pets peace and relief
For the compassion shown to us all to help us through our grief

When that time to let go weighs down your heavy heart
Picture what they are going to…. not the loss when they depart

For God's grace assures us, one day we will all meet again
When we set them free…and bear the loss…waiting until then

We can only close our eyes and imagine the look upon their face
With wagging tails and dancing feet and our sweet embrace

Our love comes full circle and deep inside we know the why
We believe in Heaven…it's an interlude and not goodbye!

Christine M. Tozzo ©2016

The Teachings of Hope...

She appeared, in an instant...out of the corner of my eye
A dog alone, on a dark country road, of course we could not pass her by
As I opened the door, she crawled, so slowly across my lap
We knew that we had to help her...not knowing what else was on tap

Her eyes were runny she was covered in sores with a big lump on her ear
We did not know how or why but with us she had nothing to fear

My rescue helpers, Halle and Cora, accompanied me to the vet
We were sure her maladies were minor and her new future set

The skin lesions were infected which an antibiotic could surely cure
But her mast cell cancer and heart worms...were more than her life could endure

As our eyes welled with tears, realization set in with each and every word now sweet Hope will show us all...what in her death sentence needs to be heard

Her prognosis means nothing to her, for she lives for each moment of life How beautiful our lives could be if we lived, Hopes way, without strife

She now has food and shelter and loves being encircled by the arms of a child
New friends, a soft bed and room to run...safe but free and wild

We tell her she is beautiful and give her kisses, hugs and love
She has found human kindness...and it fits her like a glove
So, to the person who dumped her like trash...to die on the side of the road

To you, we can only say thank you...for the burden you sought to unload
For the gift you bestowed on our lives, we gladly and humbly agree
Has taught us that Hope is eternal...and that love ALWAYS sets us free!

Christine M. Tozzo ©2019

My Name is Khalessi

The whole world wants to know how I came this far
As they analyze each wound and count my every scar

But there are scars inside me...that no one can ever see
I have chosen to forget them now that I have been set free

When I was found, my life began and I look only to each day
So happy and so grateful to the special people sent my way

Mom and Dad and all my fans and the doctors' gentle care
Filling my life every day...with joy beyond compare

I've been treated like a Princess...at least that's what I'm told
I lap it all up with pleasure as I watch my new life unfold

I've received awards and worldwide fame...but I take it all in stride
Now that I can walk again...I strut around with so much pride

As long as I have grass to roll in...rays of sun and carrot treats
My new life is full of love...and my world feels so complete

I have a nose, I can breathe and taste each morsel I am given
Energy bursting forth through me as though I am being driven

I am racing Father Time...one day I'll see my last setting sun
I will take my last deep breath and over the rainbow bridge I'll run

But, Khalessi is my name....and it means that I am very strong

I will fight with my last ounce of strength to stay here where I belong

But, when that day is upon me...please don't fill your life with grief Remember all I taught the world who looked on with disbelief

I survived such horror and found a world of beauty and of grace
Please find another sweet lost soul...who can fill that empty space

Keep teaching other dogs that there are kind humans all around
Then tell them softly of my story...how I was lost but I was found!

Christine M. Tozzo © 2016

Life at the Pound....

Bars are all around me...just like I'm in jail
Anyone who comes my way, I quickly wag my tail

See, I sure am friendly...as sweet as I can be
Hoping they will be the one who wants to set me free

Those who take care of me are full of love and light
I can somehow tell that they understand my plight

They know my days are numbered and when I get to one
We know that my time on earth...will very soon be done

There are lots of friends around. But it is not enough
I want a family of my own. The waiting sure is tough

So can't you find it in your heart to take me home with you
I promise I'all be really good... so faithful and so true

The fee is really small...the rewards are very great
So pick ME, if you will, before it is too late

Sign the form, grab a leash and we'll be on our way
When you get me home…that's where I will stay

Always grateful for my good fortune. My heart will not forget
The others that I left behind who haven't found a family yet.

                     Christine M. Tozzo © 2016

Senior Moments

I no longer am a puppy...bright eyed and bushy tailed
My old legs don't work too well and my eyesight has failed

Sometimes the people we loved so long fail us in the end
We long for that special bond of love on which we can depend

There are Angels here on earth who step in to play that role
Reminding us of who we were as the hands of time takes its toll

We get treated with respect and they tend to our every need
Simple creature comforts...on which bruised hearts feed

We know, one day, the Rainbow Bridge will come into view
We will instantly know the why and what we have to do

Say goodbye to earthly life that failed us but left us blessed
Grateful for hands reaching out who passed God's every test

So, we thank you wondrous souls who fill in that empty void
Rekindling the light inside our hearts that someone else destroyed

Do not forget us ever...but keep finding those left behind
May God bless your path on earth with all things beautiful and kind!

Christine M. Tozzo © 2018

Notes

Hope for the Misunderstood

The Homeless Prayer…

You can ask all kinds of people and they will have a different view
About the homeless population and what society should do

Some feel their lot in life, comes from mistakes and misdeeds
They close their eyes to their plight and their endless needs

Others feel all God's people deserve a second chance
They see a soul before them caught in a spiraling circumstance

Rich or poor, homeless or not…we all belong to God
He loves us unconditionally…no matter what our facade

He gives us the choice to see through His eyes or our own
Always hopeful, with His guidance, we will do what He has shown

When times are good, we believe our feet will stay on solid ground
In an instant, lives can crumble…with a quiet or deafening sound

We have a path we follow…as we walk upon the earth
All we have and our status is no true measure of our worth

My prayer is to open eyes and hearts to those too weak to stand
We may not have a lot to give…but we <u>all</u> can lend a hand!

Christine M. Tozzo ©2015

Indifference

Indifference is like a prison…only the guilty have the key
A narrow mind is your decision…you think that's how it's meant to be

Look down upon the little people…they'all never be as good as you
Go hide inside your church and steeple…like so many people do

Justify your life with prayer…seek shelter on the Sabbath day
Indifference is everywhere…to wipe it clean you kneel and pray

What about the homeless man who begged you for a slice of bread?
Was it you who turned and ran…did he get inside your head?

Did you see the little children…playing stickball in the street?
You blew them off with words unspoken…do they have enough to eat?

What about the deal you made…through promises and little lies?
All's fair as long as you get paid …you view life through jaded eyes

Yet you say your hands are clean…Holy water made them so
On Judgment day it will be seen…when it is your time to go

Will you be judged for your attendance…or rather for your apathy?
When God calls for your repentance…will you still be too blind to see?

Christine M. Tozzo ©1995

Peace, Love, And Understanding

From the day we are born, each person's unique
In our actions and thoughts, how we look, walk and speak

We go through our lives the best way we can
Though it's hard not to question, it's all part of the plan

There are times in our lives when the going's uphill
And the road that we follow takes real strength and will

But God gives us a path and a mission on earth
And that vision begins from the day of our birth

Some walk a path that is real straight and narrow
Others challenge a world whose views are too shallow

And walk to the beat of a much different band
To find peace in a world that does not understand

By discarding the stigma of our outer facade
Knowing we all are creations of God

We can break down the walls of views set in stone
And reach out our hands to those standing alone.

Christine M. Tozzo © 1995

Reaching Out

Where am I going…and how will I get there
Is a question that's asked every day
As teenagers' lives abound in confusion
Their lives are a portrait in gray
Absentee fathers, full-time working mothers
Peer pressure from every side

As their see saw emotions rise up and slam down
And they fight to hold onto their pride
But some are quite lucky to have cross their path
A person who sees through their pain
Who knows reaching out with some compassion
Brings sunshine when there's only rain

My hope for all children is answers and exits
When there are doors slamming shut every day
In their world of confusion let's open some windows
So each lost child can still find their way!

Christine M. Tozzo © 1995

The Lonely Place…

Loneliness is an ache deep within your soul
A feeling of utter sadness…in a life out of control

Feelings of self-loathing…all part of an inner play
Swirling deep inside your mind as though there is no other way

The dark abyss grows deeper and you try your best to hide
Sure that the world can see the battle raging deep inside

Like a lone set of footsteps walking toward the sea
No matter how hard you try only dark skies can you see

If the only light before you is dim and barely there
There is help right at your side though you are unaware

God is waiting for the chance for you to feel His love
Open up your eyes and look to Heaven up above

He wants to release you from the bonds and chains
Bring you forth into the light…where his pure love reigns

So close your eyes and pray…feel His love deep and true
Then walk in the sunshine… see the beauty awaiting you

Every step you take will be propelled by God's grace
The darkness you once knew…filled with God's light in its place.

Christine M. Tozzo © 2015

Expectations and Realizations

Some walk through life on golden streets and never deal with pain
Others brace for storms and wind and shelter from the rain

God is always in control and our souls know the path
Every trial and tribulation and the resulting aftermath

What we might see as darkness is our pathway to the light
Although it's hard to find our way and keep our faith in sight

We may lose a precious someone but gain an Angel as a guide
One door may close on love and then another opens wide

If we try to see the beauty of every day we are here on earth
Knowing that our lives twists and turns were determined right from birth

When people break our heart…it's a tough lesson to learn
Then we meet a perfect stranger who shows compassion and concern

God gives us a path we follow and we sometimes go astray
Praying we find our destined path and be grateful for each day

The ebb of life rolls in and out like the waves on a stormy sea
As we learn how to bridge each up and down we are finally set free
Let's be grateful for each moment and remember we are blessed
When our time on earth is over…we'll know we passed God's every test!

Christine M. Tozzo © 2015

Giving Hands and Hearts...

There are many people who can simply turn away
When they are faced with suffering and hurt day after day
Others seems to have the knack of knowing what to do
Reaching out to broken hearts and striving to break through

Giving hands holding on...to those too weak to stand
Kind words and simple deeds that calm the shifting sand
It only takes a little bit of time and faith and trust
Many joining in together to accomplish what they must

Golden hearts at work create a rainbow all their own
The most beautiful kaleidoscope the world has ever known
Selfless acts of kindness speak volumes to those in need
A rippling of grateful hearts who know they were blessed, indeed!

Christine M. Tozzo © 2009

Notes

Ecology and Change

Stop, Look and Listen!

The windswept rain in the dark of night
An eagles strong majestic flight
These miracles of sound and sight
Take my breath away.

The crashing of the waves to shore
The lightning's flash…the thunder's roar
A rainbow's gift from storms before
Takes my breath away.

Sunlight dancing on the sand
The beauty of God's open land
Mother Nature's desperate stand
Before the beauty's gone away

Poisoned by the works of man
We must act soon with mighty plan
To protect our earth while we still can
Before IT takes our breath away!!

Christine M. Tozzo © 1995

The Earth's Prayer

This beautiful globe that sustains us each day
Is fighting pollution caused by what we throw away

Scattered litter and chemicals on land and seas
Streams filled with rubbish...and poisons in the breeze

Chemical warfare and not enough safe places for trash
Our skies holding toxins... released in a flash

Searching what can be done with each ecological solution
To stop acid rain ... chemical dumps and pollution

We can each do our small part by being mindfully aware
That there are way too many people who just don't care

The sides of the roadways that people simply discard
Their bottles and plastics...why for them is it hard?

To recycle and try to honor our earths silent plea
Clean up what you cause...and the trash that you see

If we work together we can do our part of His plan
To restore what God gave us. Please do all that you can!

Christine Tozzo © 2024

The Winds of Change…

We have become complacent to all that we hold dear
Believing "this too shall pass" dismissing all the fear

The headlines post the photos that are so hard to ignore
The beaches tell the story as sea life lays dying on the shore

Where are the environmental groups who study the ocean's pulse?

Who did not foresee this toxic bloom and the disastrous, sad result

This is not a temporary problem that will be swept out of sight
It is a screaming wakeup call…to the victims' desperate plight

We love this land we call home and ocean dwellers deserve the same
It is not a time for pointing fingers and deciding who's to blame

We are all polluters and yet we can all learn to be a part
Of the solution to this heartache…with education as a start

Praying for a gathering of hearts and minds to lend a hand
To restore the beauty, we once knew. To our oceans, sky and land

Knowledge is the power and together our voices will be heard
We will speak for the voiceless…every sea creature and bird!

Christine M. Tozzo © 2018

The Eye of the Storm

Changes are whirling as the summer storm nears
The tension is rising…but only she hears

Emotions are crashing like waves to the shore
The sound too familiar…she's been there before

She fights to stay strong in the unyielding path
Praying she survives the storm's mighty wrath

When the storm has subsided and the rains gone away
Can she pick up the pieces and start a new day?

Or will she be a victim of the wind and the rain
Stripped raw of emotion…in a deluge of pain

The weather forecasters predict what they will
In the eye of the storm her world's very still

She's longing for blue skies and the rainbows storms bring
Like a cold starving sparrow…awaiting the Spring.

Christine M. Tozzo ©2009

Poisoned Promises

What will we tell the children
How can we explain
About the Earth of yesterday
Now destroyed by acid rain;

The lakes and streams all poisoned
By chemicals and trash
Each day the fish are dying
As quick as the lightening's flash;

For all our lazy habits
How Insensitive we were
The deep blue skies of long ago
Are now a hazy blur;

We're all guilty of pollution
With our lack of care and greed
For our selfish misconception
Is we can take more than we need;

What about the future
Who will undo all this mess
Like a gaping wound without a suture
I have no answers, I confess.

Christine M. Tozzo ©1995

Notes

Frustration and Realization

Black and White

There's such a fine line between love and hate
Just a glimmer of hope between go and wait

We pattern our lives in all shades of gray
With our rose-colored glasses, we greet each new day

It might take a week or a month or a year
Until your vision becomes crystal clear

It's then you'll see that something's not right
And your focus will change to pure black and white

So keep your eyes open...to your own self be true
For a heart cannot love when it's all black and blue!

Christine M. Tozzo © 1995

The War

There's a war that we wager…each and every day
Memories of hurtful things…. that just won't go away

A childhood full of sadness that lies deep within our soul
Tragedies and angry words can take their daily toll

We try to push the past aside and hold our heads up high
Tripping over past regrets and things we didn't try

When the dark clouds block your vision of who you want to be
And those around you cannot comprehend and cannot see

Your heart and soul are beautiful and if you try every day
Through dead ends and detours…you will always find your way

Words are simply vehicles and you get to choose which way to go
Discard the empty prophesies from those who just don't know

If we live our lives in weakness and never show them they are wrong
How can they know if we never show…how God has made us strong?

There is life after the loneliness…there is hope is the morning sun
Head held high…reaching for the sky…your new world has begun

Christine M. Tozzo © 2019

Pathways of Life

There are so many paths in the journey of life
Twisting highways of joy and roads filled with strife;

We go through our lives the best way we can
Though it's hard not to question, it's all part of the plan;

For god gives us a path and a mission on earth
And that vision begins from the day of our birth;

You may not understand why your blue skies turned gray
And you suffer in silence when there's so much to say;

Though it may be hard to know where to begin
By reliving the memories of where you have been;

With the help of your loved ones and those you hold dear
Standing beside you and easing your fear;

You will find the strength to do what you must do
By believing in rainbows and pots of gold, too;

Embrace all the joy of the years that have passed
And you will find inner peace and solace at last!!

Christine M. Tozzo ©2005

The Battle Zone

There's a war going on in my head and my veins
And the battle scars left are these aches and pains

You can't see the frays...they are fought deep inside
As the cowardly virus attacks and then hides

My strength has been sapped...my will compromised
This bug I am hosting is loathed and despised

When I'm back in control...healing me will begin
For I have the power to fight back and win

Those germs and invaders do not stand a chance
And one day soon I'll be doing a victory dance

Until I'm back on top and those germs gone away
I will look toward the future and each bright new day

But for now I must rest and plan my strategy
The only way I can heal. Is through God and me!

Christine Tozzo ©1996

Life's Lessons

From the day that we are born, we face many roads ahead
Paths with twists and turns and decisions that we dread

Making mistakes as we go along are the things that help us grow
We absorb the pain and heartache and follow what we know

But, our lives were not perfect and imprinted in our soul
Patterns and insecurities that through the years can take a toll

So, we lash out to another who has caused us pain and wrath
Never caring that our outburst leads us down a crooked path

Forgiveness is a virtue that few truly can possess
While grudges leave our cluttered minds in a bitter mess

We hear mental tapes from our past but if we can let go
Of those hurtful memories defining us, soon our heart will know

We can be set free if we look at the world through different eyes

Responding to pain with kindness and the path of compromise

Casting negative emotions aside is a warm blast of sanity
When the world tries to bring us down.... only love will set us free!

Christine M. Tozzo © 2015

Lifeline

They say they'll cut me down to size
I think I'm fine the way I am
The world views me through jaded eyes
And I'm their sacrificial lamb

I endure the daily pain
Knowing that my day will come
I leave at night in drenching rain
My savior sends the morning sun

I know not where my path will lead me
Or what will be my final fate
I only know this dream within me
And I pray it's not too late

So if you see me on the roadside
Or find me sleeping on the ground
There's a person on the inside
Who's just waiting to be found

Won't you let me walk beside you
Not behind or far ahead
I need a friend who'll see me through
My broken spirit's almost dead

We'll walk a path that's straight and narrow
I need a change of circumstance
I'll make my mark just like an arrow
Won't you please give me the chance?

Christine M. Tozzo © 1995

One Day at a Time…

Each day the sun rises as a new day is born
Awakening the heartache and the reason we mourn

For the life of a loved one who was taken one day
Gone from our vision to a place far away

We hold onto the memories, yet long for the touch
Try to hold back the tears…the ache hurts so much

Tears turn to frustration -- to anger and rage
What emotion is normal -- it is so hard to gauge

Yet, the memories and love are what carry us through
As we try new directions to see what we can do

To shield others from heartache -- to do what's in our power
To live, learn and grow -- every minute and hour

As we watch the sun set -- as each day nears its end
It's beauty and peacefulness helps us to mend

We welcome the nighttime -- as we wait for the dawn
Knowing God's love is with us -- He'll help us carry on.

Christine M. Tozzo © 1999

Time

It's something that we covet…and yet we waste away
Going through life on a rocky path, day after day

We awaken to a ticking clock like a siren screaming fire
Gather our thoughts of what lies ahead and how we can inspire

Longing for the strength to change the course from dark to light
Weighed down by the burdens of trying to do what's right

Who's to say if our path will be paved or will twist and turn
If we follow in someone one's shadow…how will we ever learn

We become a conduit of everyone's advice but not our own
Like we did in childhood…we only knew what we were shown

Held captive by the consequence we face if we are wrong
Like a broken record player…stuck on the same old song

I look to God for the courage to break free of every chain
Releasing all the hurt and words that are dancing in my brain

Seeking the strength to realize nothing will change if I never do
My suit of Armor may be tattered and my heart black and blue
But God 's word assures us he will catch us if we fall apart
It's time to put His words into action the time is now to start

Lord protect my innocence and expectations gone astray
Keep me safe from dark cruel words…for God's grace I pray!

Christine M. Tozzo © 2024

Up, Up and Away….

Some days when I arise
And I think about the day
So much work and compromise
I just want to turn away

Back to the safety of my bed
Drift off into another world
Erase the thoughts inside my head
Where my peace is unfurled

But reality contains me
From running from the task
Of all the people I must be
Each day donning a new mask

Trying to keep a world happy
When sadness is all around
Make it quick and make it snappy
Where quiet is a deafening sound

I know that I've been chosen
A chance to enrich someone's life
Tending to souls that have been frozen
Trying to lessen the fear and the strife

So up on my feet I comprise
All that can be good for a soul
Much to my continued surprise
I feel blessed in my earthly roll!

Christine M. Tozzo © 2016

When I'm Old and Gray...

What will people think of me when my time is drawing near
Will they think sweetly of my kindness...those memories so dear

Or will they remember me as selfish turning from God's way
Thinking only of myself with complaints day after day

My wish for all souls is to realize it's God's fervent will
For us to give and help others...we have an earthy void to fill

We give to church and strangers and lend a helping hand
We give to spread God's message all across the land

When tragedy strikes our lives and we are mired with grief
We must cling tightly to His promise and hold to our belief

That tough times befall us all and we weather stormy seas
Instead of crying out with wrath...He wants us on our knees

Praising Him in knowing He is always at the helm
We are here to learn and grow within our God's realm

It might be easier to be angry and ask God "but why?"
Then to know He holds the power and look up to the sky

For all things have a reason and some day we will know
When our time on earth is finished and it is our time to go

I hope we all can look back on life and smile so happily
Knowing we did our best for Him and so He set us free!

Christine M. Tozzo © 2016

If You Believe....

We awaken in the morning ready to face the day
Never knowing what obstacles might get in the way

We try to be uplifting and shed light in what we do
Trying to gauge your peers who might not believe in you

A cheery "Good Morning" might get a smirk or a frown
Insecure souls take it to heart...but don't let it bring you down

We envy those whose cheerfulness cuts just like a knife
Knowing what you have been through the pain and the strife

When our load is heavy it's hard to see life with opened heart
Remember we all have a journey each different from the start

We carry our burdens in our memories but if we can let the past go
Reach for the goodness of life...and let your kindness overflow

Whatever trials were behind you...just give them all to God
Face forward in love and grace and discard your hurt facade

The Heavens will guide you to what you deserve here and now
You say you can't be happy again...let our God show you how!

Christine Tozzo © 2023

Notes

Thank you for reading my work and I am hoping the poems were helpful and enlightening in your life. Any feedback as to the impact they had on you or help for someone you love will be encouraging and inspire me to keep writing. God Bless you!

Write me at: chriscanread@aol.com

Made in the USA
Monee, IL
26 June 2024